The Medieval Horse
Shedding Light on Horses of the Dark Ages

BROUGHT TO YOU BY

The books created by Equine Heritage Institute are designed to preserve the history and majesty of the horse. Our goal is to find, understand, and pass on the valuable data about equine use and its influence on humanity. The Equine Heritage Institute is a not for profit 503(c) and 100% of all proceeds from the sale of books, services, and products support Equine Heritage Institute's mission.

To make a donation to EHI, please visit www.ehi-donations.com

SPECIAL THANKS TO OUR TEAM

Mary Chris Foxworthy, Research Writer

Mary Chris Foxworthy's grandfather owned one of the last creameries in the United States that still used horse-drawn milk wagons. This sparked Mary's life-long love affair with horses and passion for keeping their history alive. After graduating from college with a degree in Food Science and Communications, Mary Chris bought her very first horse with her very first paycheck. Since then, she has served on the board of various equine associations and held a judge's card in Carriage Driving. She is known for her work in the Gloria Austin Collection, and has published and presented numerous equine educational programs. She has written for several equine publications and won an award from American Horse Publications for one of her articles. Mary Chris is an active exhibitor in Carriage Driving and Dressage. Along with her husband, she enjoys spending time with their horses (three Morgans and a PRE), a bouncing Bearded Collie and two adult children.

Taylor Murray, Editor

Taylor Murray is a copy editor and creative writer who currently resides in Ocala, FL; also known as The Horse Capital of the World. Taylor is a professional in the Hospitality industry as an Event Planner, but her passion has always been writing. In 2015, she graduated from Florida Gulf Coast University with a bachelor's degree in Hospitality Management and a Minor in Creative Writing. After a few years of making sure hotel rooms were booked and parties were planned, she decided to pursue her passion in writing. Since then, she has written for business websites, completed her first collection of poetry, and hopes to one day publish a novel based on her life.

Abby David, Graphic Designer

Abby David's family has roots in the Walking Horse tradition and she grew up hearing tales of Ole Tobe the mule's antics, holiday wagon decorations, and trick riding. She landed a job as a Graphic Designer at The Arts Center of Cannon County in 2004 and has worked in the print and digital mass communications industry continuously. Since marrying into a family in the racehorse business, David Racing Stables and Ortiz Racing Stables, she has enjoyed exploring a whole new world of horses and wearing big fancy hats. She also enjoys dancing in all it's forms and teaches in her local community.

Gloria Austin's Collection of Books

www.GloriaAustin.com

ENJOY OUR OTHER BOOKS

- How a Horse Can Make You a Better Dancer
- The Brewster Story
- Carriage Lamps
- Gloria Austin's Carriage Collection
- A Glossary of Harness Parts
- Equine Elegance

- The Fire Horse
- Horse Basics 101
- The Unsung Heros of World War One
- The Horse, History, and Human Culture
- Horse Symbolism
- Horses of the Americas

- A Drive Through Time: Carriages, Horses, and History
- Speak Your Horse's Language
- Tea: Steeped in Tradition
- The Golden Carriage and the House of Hapsburg

Brought To You By The Equine Heritage Institute

The Medieval Horse
Shedding Light on Horses of the Dark Ages
Equine Heritage Institute, Inc. (EHI)

First Publish Date 2019
Copyright © 2019 by Equine Heritage Institute, Inc.

All rights reserved. No part of this publication may be reproduced, distributed, or transmitted in any form or by any means, including photocopying, recording, or other electronic or mechanical methods, without the
prior written permission of the publisher, except in the case of brief quotations embodied in critical reviews and certain other noncommercial uses permitted by copyright law. For permission requests, write to the publisher, addressed "Attention: Permissions Coordinator," at the address below.

Gloria Austin Carriage Collection, LLC; Equine Heritage Institute, Inc.
3024 Marion County Road Weirsdale, FL 32195 Office: (352) 753-2826 Fax: (352) 753-6186

Ordering Information:
Quantity sales: Special discounts are available on quantity purchases by corporations, associations, and others. For details, contact the publisher at the address above.
Printed in the United States of America First Edition ISBN

Front Cover featured sculpture, 1st in Warhorse series by Douwe Blumberg

978-1-7339860-7-6 - Print,   978-1-7339860-8-3 - Ebook

Table of Contents

The Fall of the Roman Empire 8

The Dark Ages 10

Monks and their Mounts 11

Invasions and Heroes 13

Feudalism and Chivalry 18

Becoming a Knight 19

The Knight's Horse 21

Other Medieval Horses 24

Medieval Tack 30

Entertainment in the Middle Ages 32

"Vacations" in the Middle Ages 35

Trades of the Middle Ages 36

The Crusades 39

Coming Out of the Dark Ages 42

Sources 44

The Fall of the Roman Empire

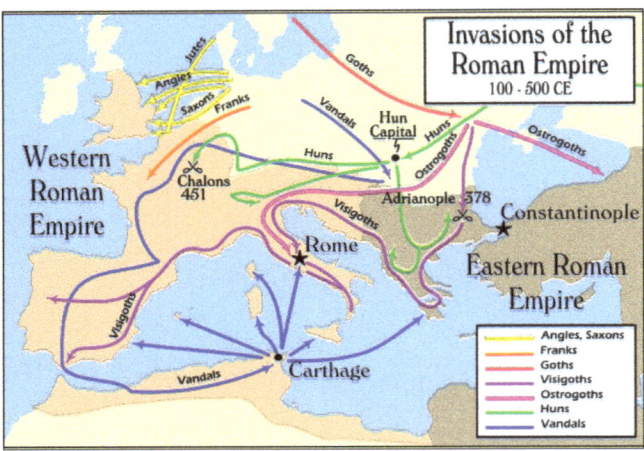

The Western Roman Empire became so vast that the Roman military could no longer protect all of the borders like they once did. Invaders with superior horsemanship skills began to continually invade from every direction. Most of the time the invaders had better horses and horsemanship skills and thus became the conqueror.

The Huns for instance, seemed as if they were glued to their saddles! Some historians mention them as doing almost everything from atop their horses; even eating and sleeping.

The Huns were taught to ride a horse as early as they could walk, at which time they were also taught how to fire a bow from atop their horse. The Hunnic bow was an engineering marvel of the time. It was a reflex bow, which means that when strung, it bent back upon itself, giving it more tension than any other bow of its time. A warrior could inflict a deadly shot at eighty yards and fire an arrow three times that distance. Unlike

the other saddles used by the Romans and other Europeans, the Hun saddles had a high front and rear section. This helped the rider to be very steady in the saddle; almost as if he was fixed to his horse. This way he could twist and turn in a three hundred sixty-degree angle without the risk of falling off, all the while firing his long-range bow in all directions. The Huns also usually made use of the lasso in battle. They would usually fight and travel in relatively small numbers, no more than a few hundred riders. If they encountered an enemy, they would dash in and strike with lightning speed and then retreat, only to reappear elsewhere and strike again.

The attacks on Rome were not over after the departure of the Huns and the Western Roman Empire officially ended in 476 AD when Emperor Romulus Augustus was overthrown by the Germanic king, Odoacer.

Augustus, the last Roman Emperor, surrenders to the Germanic king, Odoacer.

The Dark Ages

After the fall of Rome, the next period in history is often called "The Dark Ages". The Dark Ages lasted from 500 AD to 1500 AD. Instead of a single emperor ruling a vast empire, dozens of kings and princes now ruled smaller territories. Their power was based on the control of their military forces. They were not Romans; they were Anglo-Saxons in Britain, Goths in southern Gaul and Spain and Vandals in North Africa. These peoples were referred to as barbarians. They were not literate and they did not have sophisticated architecture and art. They had no written laws and they did not have an economic system.

Some people call this time period "The Dark Ages" because we do not have much information about this time in history. Since people did not write things down during this time in history, we are "in the dark" about what happened. Some people call it the Dark Ages because there were not as many innovations developed and there was little cultural advancement. Many saw it as a time of decline, since the great buildings of Rome like the Colosseum, were slowly crumbling and no one was producing great works of literature. It was an unruly time. Many roving invaders on horseback were constantly invading the countryside and, on a larger scale, there were wars and crusades.

Historians are more positive now about this period in history. This time period in history is now more often called "The Middle Ages". or "Medieval Times".

During the Middle Ages the Christian church was growing due to the missionary work of monks. Trade routes were also very busy during the Middle Ages; the world became very interconnected. There were horses used everywhere for many things.

The horse defined the Middle Ages! Horses, along with mules and donkeys, were relied on for transportation, agriculture, war and recreation. A large part of the population was dedicated to occupations that used or cared for horses.

The Duke of Brittany and his knights entering the town, preceded by the destriers' parade, Barthélémy d'Eyck, King René's Book of Tournaments, c. 1460-1465.

Monks and their Mounts

Missionary activity was common in the Middle Ages. Many who sought to dedicate their lives to the Church went to study, live and work in the monasteries. Over time monks, who normally stayed in their monasteries praying, became missionaries too. Monasteries became centers of learning. Priests often traveled between churches and monasteries preaching. Monasteries also welcomed travelers; it was an opportunity for the monks to teach their visitors about Christianity.

Monasteries often had stables for the horses of their guests. Many monasteries also kept their own horses so that they could travel and preach as needed.

Missionaries often had to travel long distances over uncertain roads so smooth-gaited horses were preferred. Palfreys, also known as Jennets, were a type of horse that could do a smooth, ground-covering four-beat gait, known as an amble, rather than the more jarring trot. In the Middle Ages horses were categorized based on type and what they could do; they did not have breeds of horses in the early Middle Ages. It is likely that missionaries had Palfreys. Palfreys were very valuable horses in the Middle Ages! The monk in Chaucer's "Canterbury Tales "rode a Palfrey.

Monk from Chaucer's "Canterbury Tales on a Palfrey

The great barn at Abbotsbury is the only surviving building of St. Peter's Abbey in Abbotsbury. The abbey was founded in 1040.

Later in the Middle Ages people became interested in breeding horses in order to produce horses that were best for the specific needs.

Horses were bred by Carthusian Monks beginning in the late Middle Ages. Some of the earliest written pedigrees in recorded European history were kept by the Carthusian monks. Since they could read and write, they kept careful records. They used the finest Spanish Jennets as a foundation for the horses they were breeding. How did the monks start breeding such amazing horses? One story says that a man named Don Pedro Picado, was unable to pay his rent to the monks so he decided to pay them by offering them his mares and colts. At the same time the monks also bought a stallion from a soldier. One of its sons, a colt of extraordinary beauty and grace, was called "Esclavo" and he was used for breeding too. The horses bred by the monks were highly sought after by many people, including kings! Through the years the Carthusian monks guarded their bloodlines with passion, even denying an order to breed horses owned by royal stud farms into their stock!

About eighty-two percent of the Pura Raza Espanola (PRE) horses in Spain today contain some Carthusian blood.

Mural in Castello Pandone Venafro, Italy

Invasions and Heroes

When Rome controlled Britain, they never really controlled all of Britain. Britain had many tribes of Celts and each tribe had a different king The people who lived in Britain at the time were called Celts. When Rome controlled Britain, they never really controlled all of Britain. Britain had many tribes of Celts and each tribe had a different king.

Horses had great importance in the religion and culture of the people at the time so it was common to tell stories giving horse names and characteristics to the people in the stories. When the Germanic tribes invaded Britain the Angles, Saxons and Jutes who lived there were said to have been led by two legendary brothers named Hengist (the name means stallion) and Horsa (the name means horse).

It was also said that the invaders of Britain had a banner with a white horse. Many believe that it represented the mythical horse Sleipner, which belonged to the god Odin. Even today the flag of Kent County in England features a white horse. Some historians believe there may even have been an Anglo-Saxon cult of the horse. Sutton Hoo, near Woodbridge, Suffolk, is the site of two sixth and early seventh century cemeteries where horses and soldiers are buried together.

Sutton Hoo, near Woodbridge, Suffolk, is the site of two sixth and early seventh century cemeteries where horses and soldiers are buried together.

The people of Britain needed a hero to save them so the famous legend of King Arthur originated during this time.

As the terror of constant invasions spread throughout the south of Britain, many people fled across the Channel, but not all. Some stayed and fought back. These were led by a Romano-British man by the name of Ambrosius Aurelianus. In the sixth century, Gildas the Monk wrote a history of the time and he said that Ambrosius was "brave on foot, but he was braver still on horseback."

The leading people in the military at the time were in the cavalry. The soldiers on horseback had the ability to respond quickly to the constant and sudden invasions. In the Roman army, the supreme commander of Roman forces had the title of Magister Militum: "Master of Soldiers". He was assisted by a second-in-command, titled Magister Equitum: "Master of Horse." Ambrosius was formerly a Roman soldier so he most likely organized his forces the same way. He would have been the "Master of Soldiers" and he would have had a "Master of Horse". This person would have been in charge of the cavalry force that quickly responded to the invasions.

Could Ambrosius' Master of Horse been King Arthur? Some people think so. King Arthur is the king who formed the Knights of the Round Table. He was just the kind of hero the people of Britain needed! But did he really exist? Many historians have tried to prove that the stories about King Arthur are true and not a legend but it is hard since there is not much written history from the time.

Other parts of Europe were also facing invasions. The Muslim governor of Tangier, Tariq ibn Ziyād, defeated Roderick, King of Spain, on July 23, 711 AD. Roderick perished in the fight. Tariq marched straight through Spain. The people of Spain could not fight them off and Spain became a Muslim country. It was not until 1094 that there was finally a leader named El Cid who was instrumental in the Reconquest of Spain.

Charles "The Hammer" Martel at the Battle of Tours

The Islamic army invaded France too. But France had a commander in charge the likes of which the Muslims had not yet seen. His name was Charles "The Hammer" Martel. He knew that he needed an army to fight off the Islamic army and raising an army took money. He went to the Catholic church to ask for money. The Church knew that the threat of the Islam army invading the area was very dangerous; the Muslims destroyed churches wherever they went and did not allow people to practice any faith but that of Islam.

During the Battle of Tours Charles organized a secret mission and went behind the enemy lines right into the Muslim camp. He took back all of the plunder that the Muslims had stolen. The Muslims retreated. This battle was not the end of Martel's battles with the Muslims.

More invasions followed, the most serious being a fleet of ships in 736 AD. Martel was once again equal to the task of crushing these invaders. Winning battle after battle with a combination of infantry and heavy cavalry, Martel's army defeated the Muslims again and again until their final destruction at the Battle of the River Berre in 737 AD. His revolutionary heavy-cavalry tactics would define warfare for hundreds of years to come as knights lead thunderous charges on horses. Charles Martel's grandson, Charlemagne, would also
become a great ruler.

In 978 AD the Muslims, under a new ruler, begin to tax and persecuted the Christians in southern Spain. The Christians escaped to northern Spain. They joined together with the other Christians living there and decided to reconquer Spain from the Muslims. Ferdinand I, the king of Castile, in northern Spain, had a very strong army and they were able to defeat many Muslims. The Muslims knew they needed help, so they asked Muslims from North Africa to come and help them. The Muslims defeated the army of Castile and the Christians felt that they would never be able to finish their Reconquest of Spain. But Spain had a secret "weapon" - a man named El Cid.

El Cid's real name was Rodrigo Díaz de Vivar. As a young boy he was a ward of Prince Sancho, King Ferdinand's oldest son. Rodrigo was trained to be a knight by Sancho. When the Muslims defeated the army of Castile, Alfonso, the King of Spain at the time, asked El Cid to help him in the Reconquest of Spain. El Cid put together an army of four thousand and defeated the much larger army of the Muslims in 1094 AD. This was just the beginning of the victories over the Muslims. There were many more and eventually most of Spain became Christian again.

El Cid's horse, Babieca, is as famous as he is! Babieca came into the world spindly and weak. The monks who bred him thought he was worthless, so they named him Babieca, meaning fool or stupid. One of the monks, Pedro El Grande, named for his largeness, was the uncle of Rodrigo (El Cid). When Rodrigo was a young man Pedro El Grande told him that he could choose any horse from his fine stables to raise as his own. Much to the monk's surprise, Rodrigo picked the little weakling colt his uncle had named Babieca. As Rodrigo grew to become a fierce and well-respected soldier, Babieca grew to be a well-trained and devoted war-horse.

El Cid carried a legendary sword, almost as famous as his horse. He named the sword Tizona. During the siege of Valencia, El Cid fell in battle. The invaders, hearing of his death, gathered their soldiers and planned to take the city. Without their leader, El Cid's men feared they would lose, so they strapped El Cid's corpse to the saddle of Babieca, fixed Tizona into his hand and propped his arm toward the heavens. Babieca, well-trained in the art of war, charged on to the battlefield with El Cid. Dumbfounded by seeing their enemy risen from the dead, the enemy scattered in terror. Eventually, Spain was reclaimed. After the death of El Cid, Babieca was never ridden again and died two years later at the age of 40, a remarkably long life for a horse who'd seen so many battles.

In 1066 AD the King of England was Edward the Confessor, a descendant of Alfred the Great. He had been king for twenty-four years and, despite being married, he had no descendants to become king. Since he had no children, Edward promised the throne to his cousin, William, Duke of Normandy. Edward's wife and her family did not like that idea. His wife, Edith, was the daughter of the country's most powerful families, the Godwinesons.

Edward died on January 5, 1066 AD. His brother-in-law, Harold Godwinson, claimed the throne, insisting that the old king had made him king in his dying moments. That met with challenges. William, Duke of Normandy, landed at Pevensey in Sussex in September and there was a great battle - the Battle of Hastings. There is a famous tapestry, called the Bayeux Tapestry, that tells the story of the battle.

When it came to battle tactics, the two sides at Hastings had very different ideas. The English, after centuries of fighting against Vikings, fought in Scandinavian fashion, standing on foot and forming their celebrated "shieldwall" which was like the wedge of the Vikings. The Normans, by contrast fought on horseback! They also had more archers than than the English. The Bayeux Tapestry (right) shows that King Harold was hit in the eye with an arrow or… he might be the one being run down by a Norman knight. At any rate, he was killed in the battle, the Normans won, and they gained control of England.

William became known as "William the Conqueror." Many Normans now came into England and changed everything about the way the people in England had been living.

"William the Conqueror", Duke of Normandy,

The Bayeux Tapestry depicting King Harold's death during a battle with the Normans.

Feudalism and Chivalry

Until the Norman invasion, the people in England lived on their own farms. They owned the land they lived on. William said that he conquered the land and it ALL belonged to him. He divided the land up and gave it to the knights who had helped him conquer the land. These knights became known as lords. The lords gave some of their land to other knights who would fight for them. They also gave land to peasants and serfs who had to give part of everything that they raised on the land to their lord. Everyone in England served someone else; this system is called feudalism. The peasants did not like this and started to riot so the lords built big stone castles to keep themselves safe.

Knights were expected to behave according to the code of chivalry. The word "chivalry" comes from the French word "chevalerie", meaning "horse soldiery". There really was no actual written code, but it was understood by all people who lived in the Middle Ages that chivalry was a moral system which went beyond rules of combat. Knights were to have qualities such as bravery, courtesy, honor and gallantry toward women.

LA CHEVALERIE. — Armement d'un Chevalier.

Becoming a Knight

Training to be a knight started when boys were very young. The son of a knight did not usually go to school. Until a boy was seven, he might be taught a little by his mother at home or by a priest. Then he would be sent to live in the castle of another knight as a page. A page had to learn how a castle was run. He also learned how to ride well and to handle weapons.

Knight in training.

When he was fourteen, if his master was pleased with him, the page might become a squire. The word 'squire' comes from the French word 'escuyer' meaning 'shield-carrier'. The young squire learned about how to be a knight by going with his master to war and tournaments, carrying his shield, helping him put on his armor before the battle and looking after his horses.

The squire had to keep his master's equipment ready and bring it to him when it was needed, even in the midst of a battle. By the time he was twenty-one, the squire might be made a knight, and hope to be given some land by his lord.

Squire and Knight in The First Crusade.

Knights were always "in training." They needed to be prepared for a possible battle or war at all times. That was their job! The daily life of knights started at dawn when they would go to Mass. Knights took time to pray several times a day. Throughout the day the knights would discuss battle tactics and strategies among themselves. In the morning knights would engage in weapons practice at the quintain and the pell. The pell was a post in the ground that the knights used to practice striking with their swords. They practiced with wooden swords that were four times heavier than their real swords so that they could develop upper body strength. They also used the pell to practice throwing spears, battle axes, hammers and other weapons.

A quintain was used to help train a knight in the use of the lance. It consisted of a shield and dummy which suspended from a swinging pole. When the shield was hit by a charging knight the whole apparatus would rotate. The knight's task was to avoid the rotating arms and not get knocked from the saddle.

In the afternoon, a knight worked on increasing his skills in horsemanship or he would go hunting or inspect the estate with the lord he served.

The quintain and the pell.

The Knight's Horse

During the Middle Ages, horses were classified by their use, not by breed like we do today. The most valuable horse in the medieval stable was the horse of the knight, the "destrier." The word destrier, meaning "right-handed" comes from the fact that the knight held a lance under his right armpit, passing it over the horse's neck on its left side in order to hit his opponent.

The horse needed very special training too! The horse needed to run directly towards another rider. That is a very unnatural thing for a horse. The horse also had to learn to gallop on the right lead. That means that the right front leg advances and touches the ground to a greater extent than the left one. This was necessary so that the horse could be ready for an impact coming from its left. The momentum of the moving horse actually gave the blow its power so it was important that the horse was fast as well as strong so that he could accept the blows as well as help his rider deliver the blows.

The destrier was a very valuable horse so the knights even had rules to protect their horses. In tournaments, there were penalties if a horse was purposely hurt by an opponent. The horses of the knights were so valuable that they wore armor too in order to protect them from injuries. The armor for a horse was called barding. The horse helmet was called a chamfron and was designed to protect the face. The segmented plates covering the neck were called the criniere. The breastplate or peytal covered the shoulders and chest and the croupiere covered the hindquarters

No Barding

Common Barding

Full Plate Barding

For tournaments, the armor was covered with colorful embroidered cloths that identified the knight by his heraldic emblems. These coverings were known as caparisons.

There is a general misconception that these horses must have been massive but they weren't. If you go to a museum and see some actual armor from the Middle Ages, you will be surprised that the horses were no bigger than most riding horses today; the destriers were about fifteen to sixteen hands. That may seem small but that is still larger than most of the other horses of the Middle Ages. Most horses in the Middle Ages were the size of large ponies.

Armor Caparisons

Armor Caparisons

Other Medieval Horses

In the Middle Ages roads were no more than dirt tracks that often turned into mud. Some goods were carried by pack horses and carts. Men traveled on horseback and ladies traveled in wagons covered in painted cloth. The wagons looked pretty, but they were very uncomfortable on bumpy roads since wagons of the Middle Ages had no springs. Travel in the Middle Ages was very slow; they could only travel thirty to forty miles a day.

Horses were not yet classified as breeds, but referred to as types and each type had a different use. Knights only used the destrier for battle and tournaments. Most knights also had other horses. Coursers were light, fast horses. They were the most common medieval warhorses. They were more expensive and better quality than rounceys, but not as expensive as destriers. Coursers were sometimes preferred over destriers in battle. The courser was better for hard battle and fast pursuit because of their speed and stamina.

Coursers were also used for hunting. Hunting was reserved for the noble class. Often times animals were hunted with dogs that were scent or sight hounds, depending on the animal they were hunting. The most popular hunted animals were deer, boar, wolves and hares.

The rouncey was the most affordable horse and usually the animal of choice for a poorer knight or squire. Rounceys were rather plain, general purpose horses who were also used for riding and as pack horses but never for pulling carts. They could also be trained for war. Rich knights supplied their attendants with rounceys. They varied greatly in characteristics; virtually any sound and reasonably fast horse was called a rouncey.

Hawking was also a popular form of hunting. Hawking or Falconry was the sport of hunting small wild game or birds with trained birds of prey like hawks, falcons and eagles

Coursers were used as messenger horses too. Messengers were a vital link to court and government communication. They accompanied envoys to court, and they apprehended criminals so they would need a good fast horse for all of that.

The most valuable and ideal riding horse was the "palfrey". Palfreys could equal a destrier in price, and for good reason; they had an extra gait known as the amble, which was fast, comfortable, and could be maintained by both rider and horse over long distances. This made traveling much easier and more pleasant. They were usually small horses, probably no taller than fifteen hands. The horse of choice for noble ladies, the palfrey was probably quite pretty. It was used almost exclusively by nobility because of its high price tag. Palfreys are also sometimes called Jennets.

Food and goods in the Middle Ages were all transported by either pack horses or cart horses. The pack horse was faster than the cart horse, so it was used to transport perishable goods. The "sumpter" was a grade horse used as a pack horse. Knights even used sumpters to carry their armor when it was not being used. Most people think these horses were very small – pony size. There aren't that many illustrations of sumpters but in England today there are plenty of native ponies that were used extensively for hauling on the pack routes. The "hobelar" was a rugged and hardy pony which later became known as a "hobby" horse; they were also used as cart horses.

The highest demand for cart horses was the transportation of hay and timber. Unlike pack horses, cart horses were used to move bulky or oddly shaped items. Cart horses were very important for moving goods around the cities. Most carts were light, two wheeled vehicles.

In the beginning of the medieval era, the horse played only a small part in heavy farming duties. Oxen were preferred due to a lack of appropriate harnessing systems for horses. The Chinese invented the full collar harness in 100 BC but that invention did not make it to Europe until 700 AD! The full collar was one of the most important inventions in human history. It allowed the horse to maximize its pulling power by better load distribution. Now the faster horse could be used for farming.

At first, horses and oxen were commonly intermixed. Innovations such as horseshoes, whipple trees, tandem harnessing, traces and better vehicle design helped to increase wider spread use of all horse teams. The ox was stronger, cheaper to maintain and less temperamental but it lacked speed and endurance.

The horse could work fifty percent faster and up to two hours longer a day since they didn't need to rest to digest food.

The horse used for farming was called an "affrus" or "stott." They were usually smaller and cheaper than the cart or pack horse.

While oxen were not completely replaced, the horse nevertheless prevailed. By using the faster horse in combination with an improved plow and better farming practices, peasants could produce a surplus. Having a surplus enabled peasants to trade at markets on weekends. Markets then evolved into towns. Towns allowed people to give up farming and allowed a living by buying and selling surplus goods. There was a belief that, "the city air makes you free." Eventually more people did not need to live by subsistence farming. This led to the growth of cities and allowed the development of early industry, education and the arts.

While life on the farm was improving, transportation by wheeled vehicle was not. Most people in the Middles Ages either walked, rode or used a litter. There was little need for road networks in a rural, feudal and self sufficient society. The roads that did exist were not maintained; they were overgrown, dry and dusty in the summer and quagmires in the winter.

Wheeled transport was uncomfortable and more strenuous than riding horseback since the body of the vehicle sat directly on the axle. Consequently, transportation by wheeled vehicle was at a very slow pace. Furthermore, in the medieval mindset, it was an insult to manhood to ride in a carriage. Only women, the infirmed or the dead rode in carriages. A journey by carriage was dangerous since the slow moving vehicle was subject to robbers and the horses risked broken legs on the bad road.

Nobles traveled a lot during the Middle Ages. When they traveled, they took everything with them from one place to another. Sometimes they would need as many as four hundred horses to move themselves and everything they needed for a long trip!

Medieval Tack

Until the late 13th century, bridles generally had a single pair of reins; after this period it became more common for knights to to use two sets of reins, similar to that of the modern double bridle. Often at least one set was decorated.

Many of the bits used during the Middle Ages resemble the bradoon, snaffle bit and curb bit that are still in common use today. However, they often were decorated to a greater degree.

Medieval Horse Bridles

The saddle with a solid tree provided a bearing surface to protect the horse from the weight of the rider. The Romans are credited with the invention of the solid-treed saddle. Early medieval saddles resembled the Roman "four-horn" saddle and were used without stirrups.

One of the most important advances in military technology came with the invention of the stirrup. The stirrup allowed warriors on horseback to use the power of horse and rider to deliver more powerful spear thrusts from a mounted position. This seemingly small invention revolutionized military strategy and techniques on the medieval battlefield. Stirrups are a Chinese invention of the fifth century, possibly even earlier. Historians and archaeologists debate when they actually arrived in Western Europe. It is known however that at the time of Charles Martel, in the early eighth century, the verbs insilire and desilire, used in reference to getting on and off horses, were replaced by scandere equos and descendere, referring to the fact that someone must step when mounting or dismounting as opposed to leaping.

  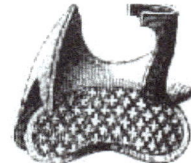

Solid-Treed Saddle

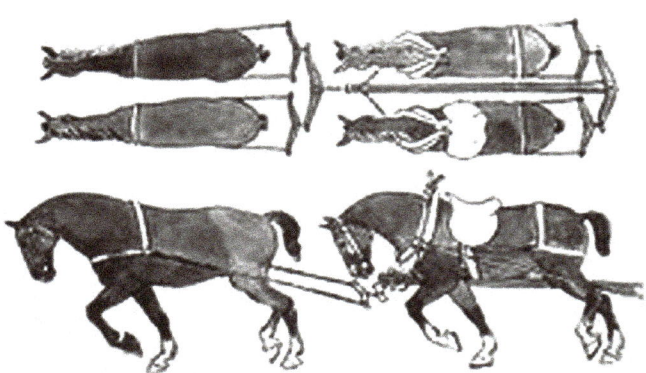

A significant development which increased the importance and use of horses in harness, particularly for ploughing and other farm work, was the horse collar. The horse collar was invented in China during the fifth century, arrived in Europe during the ninth century and became widespread throughout Europe by the twelfth century. It allowed horses to pull greater weight than they could when hitched to a vehicle by means of yokes or breast collars used in earlier times.

Heraldry, or coat-of-arms, were vitally important in Europe throughout the Middle Ages. Heraldic emblems were used to identify noble families, cities, regions and even countries. Heraldry was often used on horse equipment. Harness pendants would have been attached to a headstall, bridle or other straps. Many harness pendants also have decoration that is simply ornamental.

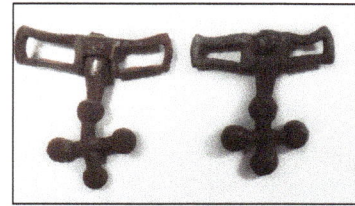

Pendants and mounts for the horse of an English bishop, circa 1250.

Heraldry Harness Pendants

Harness Pendant depicting an 'A', 14th 15th c.

Entertainment in the Middle Ages

During the Middle Ages mêlées and tournaments were the ultimate form of entertainment. It was all about horses - just like the chariot racing of the ancient Romans! Unlike chariot racing, where the men driving the horses were mostly slaves, the horsemen at the tournaments were the knights and nobles.

Early war games between rival knights and soldiers were called béhourds. These tournaments would be hosted by wealthy nobles. They were very unorganized. Many knights suffered bad injuries or were killed. The nobility who hosted these events realized there was a need to create organized events so that the fights could be more competitive and evenly matched in a safer environment. This led to the creation of medieval tournaments in which a mock battle, called a mêlée and a joust, a one-to-one mounted contest, took place.

The tournaments were considered training exercises for the knights. They were very extravagant and designed to engage the audience with an exciting display of skill. In the days leading up to the event, knights would arrive either alone or with a group. As the day of the tournament approached, stands for spectators were put up around the main stage and people began to arrive to enjoy the pre-tournament exhibition events. These events allowed individual knights to showcase their personal skills and talents.

A standard tournament involved knights divided into two teams. The tournament would begin with a review. Each side would ride out in parade fashion.

As the tournament began, two lines of knights would charge at each other on cue, with lances out. The initial charge was orderly; however, the mêlée would rapidly evolve into small groups or individual fights. The two teams continued in this fashion, each attempting to weaken or best the other, until nightfall or until they wore out. A banquet and ceremony would follow the tournament, and prizes would be awarded to the knight deemed best on each side. The host supplied food and drink for the banquet. Dancing, music and socializing played a large part in the evening's festivities as well.

The competitions were not intended to be violent or dangerous; instead, they were designed as skill tests and displays of technique and talent. But tournaments often resulted in many injuries and even fatalities, despite the presence of medieval physicians on site at all times

In 1130 AD Pope Innocent II proclaimed tournaments against the Church. He proclaimed that nobody could participate in a tournament or even attend a tournament. He also said that if anyone was killed in a tournament that they could not have a Christian burial. He felt that in glorifying warfare as entertainment, knights and villagers alike would not understand the real and important need to go to war to preserve and maintain religious ideals.

Jousting was originally only intended for pre-tournament and post-tournament exhibitions. Jousting was never intended to be the main attraction of a tournament. As mêlée type tournaments continued to be frowned upon though, jousting tournaments rose in popularity to take the place of mêlées. By the 1200s more and more tournaments featured individual fights instead of the earlier mêlée style fights. Knights were using

more ornamental armor and less dangerous weapons too. Jousts are an elimination type event. That means that the last one standing is the winner. In a jousting tournament, horses charge down tracks that are called lists. The knight would use his lance and strike the shield of the oncoming knight. The desired result would be to unseat the challenging knight to gain the highest number of points. Four charges could be made in one jousting match and a knight could also gain points for the best jousting techniques. Three jousting sticks could be used for each jousting match.

Since tournaments were intended to be entertainment and tests of skill for the knights, it was important that the horse was protected. To strike a horse was the foulest and dirtiest thing and meant disqualification. The winner of the joust could take the armor and horse of the defeated. Knights would travel the tournament circuit and, if they were successful, could make quite a nice profit. For that reason, good jousting destriers were never used in warfare.

"Vacations" in the Middle Ages

The Holy Land had long been considered the Jewish homeland. It extended from modern Israel to Egypt. The Holy Land had spiritual meaning for Christians too. Jesus Christ lived, traveled, preached and died in this region. Jerusalem was especially sacred because it was in this city that Jesus died on the cross and rose from the dead. The sites that he visited, and especially the site believed to be his tomb, made Jerusalem the most important objective for medieval Christian pilgrimage. Muslims recognized that Jerusalem was the home of the Jewish and Christian faiths that believed in one God like they did. For Muslims, Jerusalem was originally the place toward which Muslims turned in prayer, until it was changed to Mecca in 602 AD. But Jerusalem was still important to Muslims because it was the site of Muhammad's night journey and ascension.

During the Middle Ages, the Catholic church was a major part of everyday life and it became the only universal European institution. It influenced all aspects of European life and encouraged people to perform astonishing acts of devotion. Among these acts of devotion to God were the pilgrimages to special holy places like the Holy Land. Pilgrimages would be like vacations today.

People of the Middle Ages wanted to see and touch places and objects that were considered holy. People could also visit holy sites to make amends for having committed sin. By doing a pilgrimage as a penance, they hoped for for the simple pleasure of traveling. A pilgrimage was an exciting, challenging opportunity to leave village life behind. For reasons of safety, pilgrims in the Middle Ages tended to do the journey in groups.

Trades of the Middle Ages

Guilds were groups of men and women that joined together for profit and mutual protection. Each guild revolved around a particular craft or the trade of a particular type of item. The guilds established standards, set prices, and determined skills. A good example of this would be a merchant guild that dealt in making saddles. Getting a job in a particular craft meant joining a guild and following the rules for craftsmanship and pricing. A young person could be given a job as an apprentice with a master craftsman. This wasn't a paid job however. It was often the case that the young person's family actually paid the master craftsman to take on the apprentice. After a period of time as an apprentice, the young person could possibly be promoted to the position of journeyman. As a journeyman, he would now become an assistant to the master and get paid. He would learn the craft more fully. Eventually, if he had acquired the necessary skills, and had the money to pay his guild dues, he could in turn become a master craftsman. This application to become a master craftsman often had some kind of a test where the journeyman would make something that showed he had fully mastered all aspects of the craft. Many of the guilds of this era still exist today!

A large part of the population was dedicated to occupations that used or cared for horses and there were guilds for many of these occupations.

Armorers
Armorers made the custom armor for each knight. As you can imagine, this had to be done with great skill so that the it would fit the knight so that he could move and ride a horse!

Blacksmith
The blacksmith was the metalsmith. He had to first make his tools before he could make metal parts such as horseshoes, nails and door hinges. The blacksmith would also make metal weapons.

Constable
The nobles with large households would employ a constable - the "count of the stable". This person was responsible for the military protection of the household and chivalrous events such as tournaments.

Farrier
The farrier was a very important job. Not only did he put shoes on horses but he also did all the general horse "doctoring" since there were no veterinarians at the time. Henry de Ferraris received his last name from being entrusted by the king, William the Conqueror, with overseeing the work of the farriers.

Loriner
Metal parts on saddles, bridles, harnesses, spurs, stirrups and other items of horse "clothing" were supplied by the loriners' guild (the word "loriner" comes from the French word "lormier," meaning "bridle"). The Worshipful Company of Loriners, in London, was one of the first guilds in the historical record. It was created in 1261. It still exists today!

Messenger
Messengers were representatives of the lord. They carried receipts, letters and supplies. The occupation of a messenger was often dangerous. If the message was not a good one, the messenger was often the victim of the anger of the recipient leading to the saying, "Don't kill the messenger."

Saddler
The saddler made – saddles! There are still saddlery guilds today in England that existed during the Middle Ages. The Worshipful Company of Saddlers is a guild of saddlers thought to have been an Anglo-Saxon Craft Guild. They have been located at the same site since 1160!

Knight
The most prestigious profession was that of a knight. You would own a magnificent destrier and many other horses too. You would have a full set of armor and be called upon to go to war to defend your country or faith. You'd have a squire who attended to all of your needs and he would also take care of your horses and armor. You would also participate in tournaments and be like a major rock star or athlete today.

Squire
A squire attended to the needs of a knight. It was the duty of a squire to learn about the code of chivalry, the rules of heraldry, horsemanship and practice the use of weapons. It was also their duty to enter into the social life of the castle and learn courtly etiquette, music and dancing. The squire served in this role for seven years and became a knight at the age of twenty-one. Sometimes knighthood was conferred earlier as the reward for bravery on the battlefield

The Crusades

When the Islamic empire first took control of Jerusalem, they allowed Christians and Jews to visit the city. But then the Muslims turned against the Jews and Christians and refused to let the pilgrims enter the city. They robbed the pilgrims and they killed the pilgrims. Finally, they blocked all of the roads so that Jewish and Christian pilgrims could not visit the holy city at all.

By the end of the eleventh century about two-thirds of the ancient Christian world had been conquered by Muslims. They destroyed buildings and objects in the city of Jerusalem – including synagogues, Torah scrolls, Jewish artifacts and even the Church of the Holy Sepulcher, which was the place of the tomb of Jesus.

Finally, in 1095 the Byzantine emperor, Alexios I, sent a letter to Pope Urban II and asked the pope for military aid. Pope Urban preached a sermon at the Council of Clermont and called for a religious war. He asked for volunteers to travel to the East and fight. At some point, Christianity as a faith and a culture, had to defend itself or become Islamic. The Crusades were that defense.

Pope Urban II calling for the First Crusade in the marketplace during the Council of Clermont, France, 1095

The word crusade is actually a modern word. Medieval Crusaders saw themselves as "pilgrims" performing acts of righteousness on their way to the Holy Land. The crusading knights were wealthy men. They willingly gave up everything to undertake the holy mission. They did not expect to become wealthy going on the Crusade. Many of them returned as poor men since they had to personally pay all of their own expenses on the Crusade. They were aware of their sinfulness and eager to accept the hardships of the Crusade in order to atone for their sins. Several religious knightly military orders were formed including the Knights Templar, the Teutonic Knights and the Hospitallers.

It took the crusaders two years to reach Jerusalem. On June 7, 1099 AD, the Christian army of twelve hundred knights on horses and twelve thousand foot soldiers reached the holy city. The city had huge walls protecting it so the crusaders began building three enormous siege towers. By the night of July 13, the towers were complete, and the Christians began fighting their way across Jerusalem's walls and were able to gain control of the city on July 14. Jerusalem was finally under Christian control again.

When the previously conquered area of Edessa fell to Muslims in 1144 AD, a new Crusade, the Second Crusade, was launched. It was led by two kings, Louis VII of France and Conrad III of Germany. It failed

miserably. The Muslims continued to grow in strength. Saladin was a Muslim leader who conquered much territory and united the Islamic territories all the while preaching jihad against the Christians.

The response to Saladin's victories was the Third Crusade in 1189 AD. It was led by Emperor Frederick I Barbarossa of the German Empire, King Philip II Augustus of France, and King Richard I (the Lionheart) of England. Getting the horses and supplies needed to the Holy Land was a huge undertaking. To raise funds, Henry II, Richard's father, imposed a tax on his English subjects, called the "Saladin Tax". If the subject volunteered to fight in the Crusade, he did not have to pay the tax. This tax provided cash for the everything needed for the crusaders to travel to the Holy Land. It's about three thousand miles from England to Jerusalem!

Horses were critical to the military might of the crusaders so in order to transport horses, ships had to be built specifically for this purpose. The animals were fitted into slings that prevented them from lying down. It was not an easy journey for the horses and when they arrived, they needed time to recover. Saladin knew that the only way Richard was able to get horses and supplies and more soldiers was by boat so he thought he had the advantage. Saladin said, "The sea lies between us and the Christians, there is no sea to separate Arabs who cannot be numbered."

But Saladin was wrong. The Arabs were a mix of many peoples who did not want to cooperate with Saladin so he had difficulty raising a large army.

Under Richard's leadership, the Christian forces had victory after victory, eventually reconquering the entire coast. But Jerusalem was not on the coast, so it was difficult to get his horses and supplies inland.

Eventually, Richard and Saladin formed a truce that ensured peace in the region and allowed pilgrims to safely travel to the Holy Land. In 1192 AD, because Richard could not get horses and Saladin could not get an army, that was the end of the Third Crusade.

But still, Christians did not regain the Holy Land and the True Cross so there were more Crusades after this.

Coming Out of the "Dark Ages"

China did not have to worry about Islamic invasions but in 1234 AD nomadic invaders from the north, known as the Mongols, invaded China. By 1279 AD they were able to completely overthrow the Song Dynasty.

Genghis Khan (1162 AD – 1227 AD), the ruler of the Mongols, was ruthless but he was also very intelligent. He created the largest connecting empire in all of human history. At their peak, the Mongols controlled between eleven and twelve million contiguous square miles. How did he do that? With horses of course! The key to their success was that they could move great distances in very short periods of time. Their horse archers seemed like they were coming out of nowhere! They were impossible to fight because they did not stay still long enough for any kind of engagement.

The Mongol army's battle tactics depended on their sturdy, agile and durable horses. The Mongol armies respected their horses and took care of them. Every soldier had four to six horses. That way, no one horse was ridden to exhaustion and that is why they could travel great distances; sometimes sixty to a hundred miles a day.

Mongols were nomads so they spent their lives on horseback, herding and hunting. These skills were just what they needed for warfare. The Mongol army trained every day in horsemanship, archery, hand-to-hand combat and in battle formations and drills.

Up until this time, the people who were conquered had to assimilate to the culture of the conqueror. The conqueror often destroyed all aspects of the culture they conquered. That is why the first part of the Middle Ages was called "The Dark Ages". But, when the Mongols conquered an area, they made sure to never kill the tradesmen of the area. Rather, they made sure to learn from them and gather all of the knowledge they had to continue to build the empire. Since the Mongols were nomads, the horses were very important to their lifestyle. Anthropologists and archaeologists have found that the Mongol's horses were specifically bred for their lifestyle. Domestication was not a matter of training wild horses to obey commands. Rather, domestication involved genetic changes that occurred over generations of selective breeding for particular traits such as obedience, size, or comfort for the rider.

Things around the world were starting to change. Rather than loot and destroy, conquering armies were trying to mingle and learn new things from the people that they conquer. People were beginning to assimilate into the culture and there was an exchange of ideas. A new era of cultural, artistic, political and economic rebirth was about to begin!

The horse played a pivotal role in the feudal system of the Middle Ages and in the growth of modern Europe as well. At the end of the Middle Ages cites began to develop as subsistence farming was no longer necessary for the masses. With the rise of a middle class, there was an emergence of specialized horse breeding for specific purposes just as the Mongols had been doing. Beginning in the Renaissance, horses were bred for sporting endeavors as well as for war. Horses would be ridden for pleasure and used for transportation by carriage so, horses were bred for those purposes too. Improved farming methods called for a larger and stronger horse to be developed which led to the developed of draft breeds.

The world was coming out of the Dark Ages into a Renaissance and horses were going to continue to play an important role.

Sources

https://www.ancient.eu/Roman_Empire/
http://www.britannia.com/history/biographies/ambros.html
https://www.heroicage.org/issues/4/Hunter-Mann.html
https://www.archaeology.co.uk/articles/specials/timeline/sutton-hoo.htm
https://www.britannica.com/topic/Hengist
https://www.nationaltrust.org.uk/sutton-hoo/features/the-royal-burial-mounds-at-sutton-hoo
http://www.spiegel.de/international/europe/the-anglo-saxon-invasion-britain-is-more-germanic-than-it-thinks-a-768706-2.html
https://www.historic-uk.com/HistoryUK/HistoryofBritain/Invaders/
https://www.ancient.eu/Vortigern/
https://www.uni-due.de/SHE/HE_GermanicInvasions.htm
http://www.thenagain.info/WebChron/WestEurope/AngloSaxon.html
https://www.ourmigrationstory.org.uk/oms/anglo-saxon-migrations
http://www.thefinertimes.com/Middle-Ages/christianity-in-the-middle-ages.html
https://www.heritage-history.com/index.php?c=read&author=harding&book=middle&story=monastery
http://cowboyfrank.net/fortvalley/breeds/Andalusian.htm
https://www.ducksters.com/history/middle_ages_monastery.php
http://www.dallasequestriancenter.com/medieval-horse-breeds/
http://www.spanishvisionfarm.com/Articles/Bloodlines/bloodline_all_about_cartujano.html
http://www.thefinertimes.com/Middle-Ages/christianity-in-the-middle-ages.html
http://www.vlib.us/medieval/lectures/franks_rise.html
https://www.penfield.edu/webpages/jgiotto/onlinetextbook.cfm?subpage=1680226
https://www.britannica.com/biography/Roderick
https://www.history.com/topics/middle-ages/charles-martel-repels-the-moors-video
https://www.historyhit.com/day-charles-martel-dies/
https://www.reddit.com/r/AskHistorians/comments/345ito/when_did_england_become_britain/
https://www.historyextra.com/period/medieval/battle-hastings-facts-where-why-weapons-casualties-how-won/
http://www.lordsandladies.org
http://www.thearma.org/essays/pell/pellhistory.htm
https://www.abdn.ac.uk/sll/disciplines/english/lion/training.shtml

https://mad.hypotheses.org/375
https://stores.renstore.com/history-and-biography/horses-in-the-middle-ages
http://www.ox.ac.uk/news/2017-04-18-highs-and-lows-englishman%E2%80%99s-average-height-over-2000-years-0
http://www.localhistories.org/middle.html
http://www.equest4truth.com/94-discover-equus/159-horses-of-medieval-europe
http://www.medieval-life-and-times.info/medieval-life/medieval-hawking.htm
https://stores.renstore.com/history-and-biography/hors-in-the-middle-ages
https://www.alansfactoryoutlet.com/horses-in-the-middle-ages
https://www.warhistoryonline.com/medieval/11-facts-never-knew-medieval-warhorses.html
http://defendingcrusaderkingdoms.blogspot.com/2015/05/crusader-horses-destriers-palfreys-and.html
http://livingthehistoryelizabethchadwick.blogspot.com/2009/02/horses-for-courses.html
http://www.thefinertimes.com/Middle-Ages/tournaments-in-the-middle-ages.html
http://www.medievalchronicles.com/medieval-knights/medieval-tournaments/
https://www.thoughtco.com/the-holy-land-1788974
https://www.thevintagenews.com/2017/04/14/off-to-the-holy-places-pilgrimages-during-the-middle-ages/
http://www.internationalschooltoulouse.net/vs/pilgrims/motive.htm
https://www.haaretz.com/jewish/.premium-1009-the-mad-caliph-attacks-christian-sites-in-fatimid-empire-1.5450335
https://fogandfriction.com/2015/03/23/for-want-of-horses-and-ships-social-and-economic-constraints-of-christian-and-muslim-forces-during-the-third-crusade/
http://www.bbc.co.uk/history/historic_figures/richard_i_king.shtml
https://www.angus-donald.com/history/king-richards-return-imprisonment-and-ransom/
http://www.themiddleages.net/people/richard_lionheart.html
https://www.historyextra.com/period/medieval/robin-hood-real-myths-facts/
https://www.storiestogrowby.org/story/robin-hood-and-the-golden-arrow-story-legend-stories-for-kids/
http://afe.easia.columbia.edu/mongols/china/china.htm
https://asiasociety.org/education/mongol-dynasty
https://www.history.com/topics/china/genghis-khan
https://www.historyonthenet.com/the-mongol-empires-best-weapon-the-mongolian-horse
https://www.sapiens.org/column/off-the-map/horse-domestication-mongolia/
https://www.petguide.com/breeds/horse/mongolian-horse/

http://afe.easia.columbia.edu/mongols/conquests/khans_horses.pdf
htts://www.degruyter.com/downloadpdf/j/apd.2018.6.issue-1/apd-2018-0003/apd-2018-0003.pdf
http://steventill.com/2008/06/18/the-diffusion-of-the-stirrup-into-medieval-western-europe/
The Medieval Horse and Its Equipment, C.1150-c.1450 edited by John Clark
Oakeshott, Ewart (1998) A Knight and His Horse. Rev. 2nd Ed. USA:Dufour Editions ISBN 0-8023-1297-7
Clark, John (Ed) (2004) The Medieval Horse and its Equipment: c. 1150-c. 1450. Rev. 2nd Ed, UK: The Boydell Press ISBN 1-84383-097-3
http://horsehints.org/MiddleAgesHorse.htm
https://www.metmuseum.org/art/collection/search/25452

www.ingramcontent.com/pod-product-compliance
Lightning Source LLC
Chambersburg PA
CBHW061129070526
44584CB00033B/4265